SCHOOLS AROUND THE WORLD

By Eleanor O'Connell

Gareth Stevens
PUBLISHING

Please visit our website, www.garethstevens.com. For a free color catalog of all our high-quality books, call toll free 1-800-542-2595 or fax 1-877-542-2596.

Cataloging-in-Publication Data

Names: O'Connell, Eleanor.
Title: Schools around the world / Eleanor O'Connell.
Description: New York : Gareth Stevens Publishing, 2017. | Series: Adventures in culture | Includes index.
Identifiers: ISBN 9781482455892 (pbk.) | ISBN 9781482455915 (library bound) | ISBN 9781482455908 (6 pack)
Subjects: LCSH: Schools–Juvenile literature. | Schools–Cross-cultural studies–Juvenile literature.
Classification: LCC LB1513.O54 2017 | DDC 371–dc23

Published in 2017 by
Gareth Stevens Publishing
111 East 14th Street, Suite 349
New York, NY 10003

Copyright © 2017 Gareth Stevens Publishing

Designer: Andrea Davison-Bartolotta and Bethany Perl
Editor: Therese Shea

Photo credits: Cover, p. 1 OlegD/Shutterstock.com; pp. 2–24 (background texture) Flas100/Shutterstock.com; p. 5 Syda Productions/Shutterstock.com; pp. 7, 9 Jonas Gratzer/LightRocket/Getty Images; p. 11 VCG/Visual China Group/Getty Images; p. 13 TONY KARUMBA/AFP/Getty Images; p. 15 Noorullah Shirzada/AFP/Getty Images; p. 17 Visions of America/UIG/Getty Images; p. 19 Stephen Bures/Shutterstock.com; p. 21 Juan Forero/The Washington Post/Getty Images.

Printed in China

CPSIA compliance information: Batch #CW17GS: For further information contact Gareth Stevens, New York, New York at 1-800-542-2595.

CONTENTS

Boldface words appear in the glossary.

Time for School!

Some schools around the world look different than yours. Students there may dress a bit differently, too. As you read this book, imagine what it's like to go to school in these interesting places. Did you hear the bell? It's time for school!

School Boats

Much of the country of Bangladesh in South Asia floods during the rainy season. That means many schools flood. Students miss classes and get behind in their studies. Some people thought of a way to solve this problem—floating schools!

Boat schools mean students can go to class year round. The boats even pick up students—just like a school bus. Some boats have computers powered by the sun! Boat schools can be found in Cambodia, Nigeria, the Philippines, Vietnam, and Zambia, too.

Bus Classroom

You might take a bus to school. Imagine if your classroom was a bus! A school in Shanghai, China, made a bus into a classroom. The fun idea came from a children's book. It's a great way to recycle a bus, too!

Computers to Go

In some **remote** areas of Africa, students don't have **access** to the Internet and computers. People have made large **shipping containers** into computer labs for these places! Trucks can easily move the containers to new places when needed.

shipping container

13

Open-Air Schools

In some places, there aren't enough buildings for schools. In Afghanistan, schools have been destroyed by years of war. Children often gather in "open-air schools" to learn. Sometimes they hold class in tents to hide from the sun and rain.

15

What They Wear

Many schools in Africa require students to wear uniforms. However, it's not uncommon to see students walking long ways to and from school barefoot. Sometimes, they do this to make their shoes last longer.

Even in uniform, students may show their **culture** in special ways. In the Southeast Asian country of Myanmar, students sometimes wear *thanakha* (thah-nah-KAH) on their face. *Thanakha* is a yellowish-white paste made from **bark**. It guards skin from sunburn.

thanakha

19

School's Out!

In the Southern **Hemisphere**, summer is from December until March. So students in countries there, such as Brazil, have their summer vacation during this time. Would you like to go to school in a different country? Which one? Why?

GLOSSARY

access: a way of being able to use or get something

bark: the outer layer of a tree

culture: the beliefs and ways of life of a people, group, or place

hemisphere: one half of Earth

remote: far away from other people, houses, or cities

shipping container: a large box that goods are placed in so that they can be moved from one place to another on a ship, airplane, train, or truck

FOR MORE INFORMATION

BOOKS

Chambers, Catherine. *School Days Around the World.* New York, NY: DK, 2007.

Hughes, Susan. *Off to Class: Incredible and Unusual Schools Around the World.* Toronto, ON, Canada: Owlkids, 2011.

Lewis, Clare. *Schools Around the World.* Chicago, IL: Heinemann Library, 2015.

WEBSITES

Introduction to School Life
projectbritain.com/education/index.html
Read what school is like in Great Britain.

School Years Around the World
www.factmonster.com/world/statistics/school-years.html
Find out if your school year is like the school year in different countries.

INDEX